TESTIMONIES

of the

DAILY
BREAD

Greg Holt

ISBN 978-1-0980-2770-4 (paperback)
ISBN 978-1-0980-2771-1 (digital)

Copyright © 2020 by Greg Holt

All rights reserved. No part of this publication may be reproduced, distributed, or transmitted in any form or by any means, including photocopying, recording, or other electronic or mechanical methods without the prior written permission of the publisher. For permission requests, solicit the publisher via the address below.

Christian Faith Publishing, Inc.
832 Park Avenue
Meadville, PA 16335
www.christianfaithpublishing.com

Printed in the United States of America

To my wife Phyllis and to all the pastors, preachers, family, and friends who encouraged me along my Christian journey. To God be the glory.

CONTENTS

Preface 7

Chapter 1:	The Purpose of the Daily Bread	9
Chapter 2:	Food for Our Souls	13
Chapter 3:	Our Daily Bread	17
Chapter 4:	Daily Bread Testimonies	24
Chapter 5:	Receiving Our Daily Bread (God's Word)	39
Chapter 6:	It's All in the Bread (God's Word)	44

A Prayer of Salvation 49
References 51

PREFACE

I was inspired to write *Testimonies of the Daily Bread* in 2016. I have received so many e-mails from my colleagues expressing how the daily bread are a blessing to them and their families and how it lets them share how God's Word is right on time for what they need. I give God the glory for using me in such a way. There are so many people in need of God's Word especially in today's time. I hope and pray whoever reads this book will be blessed upon measures. To God be the glory.

CHAPTER 1

The Purpose of the Daily Bread

If you can't fly then run, if you can't run then walk, if you can't walk then crawl, but whatever you do you have to keep moving forward.
—Martin Luther King Jr.

The daily bread scripture is essential to our growth; one of the most important ways that we walk with Jesus is to read and study his Word as a Christian. Daily bread devotions can help with that. The purpose of the daily bread is to help you take your next step of faith. It is that daily encouragement from scripture that will help you understand the Word of God and encourage you in your faith.

The reading of the daily bread is like taking a multivitamin; the purpose of the vitamin is to reduce levels of stress and anxiety. The B vitamins convert food into energy, keeps the nervous system functioning properly, and produces stress hormones. Taking multivitamins daily can replenish your body's supply. The Word of God through the daily bread can reduce high levels of stress and calm anxiety. Daily bread reading of God's Word can lower our blood pressure, through the scriptures; we learn that Jesus is a healer. God's Word supplies all we need on a daily basis.

Sharing the daily bread with others allows us to see God move in other people's lives, so we are to go out and share God's Word. "And the Lord said unto the servant, go out into highways and hedges, and compel them to come in, that my house may be filled" (Luke 14:23, KJV). Through the daily bread, we can make disciples. Matthew 28:19 (NIV) tells us, "Therefore go and make disciples of all nations, baptizing them in the name of the Father and of the Son, and of the Holy Spirit."

TESTIMONIES OF THE DAILY BREAD

Expecting results through the daily bread as we go through our daily routine, we can see what we have read for that day was right on time. God knows what we need and when we need it. Before we begin our day, we should pray and read scripture, because it prepares us for what we will face for the day. Satan comes to kill, steal, and destroy. I can remember a time when I read the daily bread to start my day, and before I knew it, Satan reared his ugly head. I'm not perfect, but I try to remember what the daily bread taught me and the scripture it referenced.

The purpose of the daily bread is to get you on the right track, and remember Jesus has the answers for what lies ahead. Throughout the scriptures, we see answers to our questions, problems, and how to respond to others in love. The daily bread taught me how to hold my peace at times, though it's hard, because the flesh is weak, and some people know what strings to pull. When trouble strikes, we have a variety of places to turn for help, but our first option should always be the Bible. After all, it's no ordinary book. It is the unfolding revelation of almighty God. From beginning to end, the Lord demonstrates his love and concern for his people. He gives us amazing promises and has the infinite power to fulfill them.

In the daily bread, we can find help for every circumstance of life, which is found within the scriptures. Through the daily bread, it reveals our sinful condition and God's plan to rescue us. Because of his love, grace, and mercy, he made a way to forgive sins and reconcile us to himself. We can find encouragement when we need it. When hardship comes, we'll have God's Word in our minds and hearts, and we'll know exactly where we need to go for his guidance and wisdom. Matthew 6:9–11 tells us how to pray, "Our Father, which art in heaven, Hallowed be thy Name Thy Kingdom come. Thy will be done in earth, as it is in heaven. Give us this day our *daily bread*. And forgive us our trespasses, as we forgive them that trespass against us. And lead us not into temptation, but deliver us from evil. For thine is the kingdom, the power, and the glory, forever and ever. Amen [emphasis added]."

CHAPTER 2

Food for Our Souls

For the bread of God is he who has comes down from heaven and gives life to the world.
—John 6:33

Human beings are specifically designed to eat a particular kind of soul food, God's Word. That's why in both the Old and New Testaments, God emphasized, "Man shall not live by bread alone, but by every word that comes from the mouth of God" (Deuteronomy 8:3, Matthew 4:4). When God speaks, it is much different than when you and I speak. When we speak, we describe or defend our perceptions of reality. When God speaks, he speaks reality into being. Our words describe life and action. God's Word is living and active (Hebrews 4:12)

When God speaks creation, things other than himself come into being—angels, galaxies, and gnats. But when God speaks himself, he speaks uncreated, eternal deity. That is his son, who called himself the life (John 11:17, John 14:6). This is what the Apostle John was getting at when he says, "In the beginning was the word, and the word was with God and the word was God" (John 1:1). Of course, the word is God. When God speaks himself, he cannot be any other, and when the word of God speaks, he speaks the words of eternal life (John 6:68). This is why Jesus called himself "the bread of life" (John 6:35) and said, "The bread of God is he who comes down from heaven and gives life to the world" (John 6:33).

God has given human beings one source of true soul food—his son Jesus Christ, the Word of God, God the Son, is the great promise, for "all the promises of God find their Yes in him" (2 Corinthians 1:20). He is the soul's bread, and "whoever feeds on this bread will live forever" (John 6:58). What could possibly give more hope to our sinful souls than Jesus's promises of complete forgiveness of our sins, the removal of all the Father's judgment and wrath against us, to always be with us (Matthew 28:20) and give us eternal life in God's presence with full joy and pleasures forever (Psalm 16:11)? Nothing!

These are the "precious and very great promises" (2 Peter 1:4) that are designed to nourish our souls. Once we grasp this, it helps us make sense of Jesus strange-sounding words, "Unless you eat the flesh of the son of Man and drink his blood, you have no life in you" (John 6:53). When our bodies need energy, we know that we need to eat. So we eat a variety of foods, some better and some worse sources of energy and bodily health. Our body then digests these foods and converts them into energy, and we can keep going. No food, no energy, no going on.

Our lives consist of many matters, but the foremost matter for our physical survival is food. When haven't eaten in a while, we become very clear that everything else is secondary. Only eaten food satisfies our hunger and nourishes us. Without eating, we simply can't continue to exist. In the same way, the foremost matter for believers to be healthy and grow in the divine life is to eat spiritual food. But what is the food for our spiritual life? God gave his Word to us for our spiritual food. So even more than studying the Bible, we actually need to eat it. Nothing is more important to our Christian life than our being nourished with the Word of God. Similarly, what mother would insist that her child first, above all, study hard and behave well yet never prepare food for her child to eat? On the contrary, a mother knows that the primary matter concerning her child's well-being is that the child eats nourishing food to be healthy. Then all the other things can be taken care of. In the same way, God's real concern for all of us, his children, is that we be living, full of his life, and growing in his life by eating his Word.

God gave us his Word, the Bible, not to be our textbook, but to be our food. It's full of life, having been breathed out of God himself, and his words give life. Whether we end up empty and unsatisfied after we've read or studied the Bible depends on whether we come to the Bible as life-giving, nourishing food or not, and if we view the Bible simply as a book from which we can accumulate biblical knowledge, and we don't get to the spirit and life in the Word of God, we won't receive the nourishment we need to grow in God's life and to live a normal, healthy Christian life.

CHAPTER 3

Our Daily Bread

Before we begin our day, we need to sit quietly for about thirty seconds to settle our spirit, take a few deep breaths, and get comfortable. We need to open our Bibles and read a portion of scripture, and after we read the scripture, we need to pause to think about the passage of scripture we just read. What comes to mind? What caught our attention? The passage of scripture relates to the central point of the day's meditations. We need to read it slowly and think about its meaning for you. Once or twice a week, we might memorize a passage of scripture. We should always pray before and after, mentioning people or situations that come to mind during our reflections of the daily bread. Pray that God may help you remember God's words, follow God's direction, and enforce your decision by God's power. Prayer is your channel to God's power. If possible, try to pray in a quiet, orderly place. As you practice God's words through the power of prayer, your life will be full of the fruits of the Holy Spirit (Galatians 5:22, 23).

David C. McCasland writes,

> The apostle Peter reminded first-century believers that Christlike living and effective service result from a process. He urged them to grow in eight areas of spiritual development: faith, virtue, knowledge, self-control, perseverance, godliness, brotherly kindness, and love (2 Peter 1:5–7). If you possess these qualities in increasing measure, Peter said, "You will be neither barren nor unfruitful in the knowledge of our Lord Jesus Christ" (v.8).

TESTIMONIES OF THE DAILY BREAD

God calls us to a wonderful process of learning to know him, with the assurance that it will lead to productive service in his name and for his honor.

As you write down your reflections, you will often find that many unexpected insights and new understanding come to you from God through the work of the Holy Spirit. This is the benefit of spiritual journal writing.

Use either a separate notebook or the space given in *Our Daily Bread* booklet for recording your reflections and prayer according to your convenience. Try to write down your thoughts as regularly as you can. Allow yourself to sufficiently dwell in God's grace through the work of the Holy Spirit. The Holy Spirit will fill your heart with grace, rest, and strength. At the same time, the Holy Spirit will give you God's direction and guide the decisions you make. Identify this direction, and be specific in your decisions.

Our daily bread helps us to share with other's stories about the challenge and importance of actions that reflect Christ's grace, love, and mercy to the world, standing up to bullies, serving others without recognitions, attending to the small details of daily life. In Acts 2, the early Christian community broke bread together, spent time in fellowship with one another, gave to those in need, and praised God. These actions led others to explore the way of Christ and forged the community that became the church.

When you read the Bible, it's as if you were in God's presence, and He is speaking to you through His Word. It's good to read it thoughtfully and ask the Holy Spirit to interpret any difficult passages for you. Sometimes the Holy Spirit will call a special verse to your attention and reveal its meaning to you.

The Bible is a handbook for living. It is a roadmap to heaven. Without knowledge of the Word of God in our hearts, we can make mistakes that can hurt our Christian experience.

A famous Bible translator told the story of a little girl who came to him one evening while he was in Jerusalem. She asked him if he would go with her to see her mother, who was very sick. He readily agreed to do so.

"What are you doing with an oil lamp?" he asked the child.

"We live in the old section of Jerusalem," she replied, "and the streets are narrow and dark. We will need the lamp to show us the way. Please follow me."

The little girl walked ahead of him and held the lamp low, almost touching the cobblestones, so the man could see exactly where he was placing his feet. He said later, "For the first time in my life, I realized the full meaning of the scripture, *Thy word is a lamp unto my feet, and a light unto my path*" (Psalm 119:105).

Like the light that was held closely to the ground by the child, as you study the Word of God, it can shine upon your pathway and guide you. This is how you can find solid footing to avoid many of the dangers and pitfalls that lie ahead on life's journey.

Thy word is a lamp unto my feet, and a light, etc. David was a man of very good wit and natural understanding; but he gives to God the glory of his wisdom, and owns that his best light was but darkness when he was not lightened and ruled by the word of God. Oh that we would consider this, that in all our ways wherein the word of God shines not unto

> us to direct us, we do but walk in darkness, and our ways without it can lead us to none other end but utter darkness. If we hearken not to the word of God, if we walk not by the rule thereof, how is it possible we can come to the face of God? (William Cowper)

Our daily bread devotions can reach the masses; so many people need God's Word daily in their lives. Through God's Word, we can navigate through this dark world that we live. "For I know the plans I have for you, declares the Lord, plans for welfare and not for evil, to give you a future and a hope" (Jeremiah 29:11). Yes, of course, God knows the plans he has for us. And ultimately he will give us a glorious future. But as we walk out our lives on this crazy earth, let's remember that the best growth comes through persevering through trials, not escaping them entirely. And when we learn perseverance, we find surprising joy.

> What hard thing are you currently going through? In the midst of your suffering, cling to Jeremiah 29:11, but cling to it for the right reason: not in the false hope that God will take away your suffering, but in the true,

gospel confidence that he will give you hope in the midst of it.

So how does this passage apply to you? Well, Jeremiah 29:11 must be read in the context of the whole book of Jeremiah, and the book of Jeremiah must be read in the context of Israel's story. But then all of Jeremiah and Israel's entire story must be read in the context of God's purposes in Jesus Christ. All the promises of God "find their yes in him" (2 Corinthians 1:20). If we are in Christ, then all the horrors of judgment warned about in the prophets have fallen on us, in the cross, where we were united to Christ as he bore the curse of the law (Galatians 3:13). "[And] if we are in Christ, then all of the blessings promised to Abraham's offspring are now ours, since we are united to the heir of all those promises (Gal. 3:14–29)."

CHAPTER 4

Daily Bread Testimonies

My testimony started in March 16, 1991, when I accepted the Lord as my personal Savior. I remember as if it were yesterday that the Lord Jesus had to get me to a place where he could get my attention, and I could not go anywhere. He spoke to my heart and said, "If you confess with your mouth and believe in your heart that God has raised him from the dead, thou shall be saved" (Romans 10:9). "For whosoever shall call upon the name of the Lord shall be saved" (Romans 10:13). I always remembered these scriptures, and they came to life on this day. I promised the Lord if he sees me through this trial, I'll serve him and tell others how he saved me, and I've been doing this for the last twenty-eight years as of April 5, 2019. Through God's grace, he allows me to work for a company where I can share God's Word through the *Daily Bread Devotions*. We started out with only a few colleagues, and we have grown the ministry up to at least 150 to two hundred employees who are receiving the daily bread twice a week.

Through this ministry, God is doing remarkable miracles where my colleagues are sharing their testimonies on how the daily bread is working in their lives, and that is what prompted me to write this book. God called me to the ministry to preach his Word in 2015—I was licensed on November 18, 2015. It has not always been easy, growing up in foster care, not knowing my mother or father, but God had a purpose for my life. I have received so many e-mails from my colleagues sharing their testimonies, I give God the glory, and it lets me know his Word is delivering, healing, and bringing joy into their lives. "And the Lord said unto the servant, Go out into the highways and hedges, and compel them to come in, that my house may be filled" (Luke 14:23)

Remember that God does not call the equipped—he equips the called. And as Christians, we are all called to share what Christ has done. Some of Christ's last words on earth were as follows: "Go and make disciples of all nations" (Matthew 28:19). Sharing our faith isn't just a suggestion—it's a command. And God is with us when we obey him. One of the best ways to share your faith is to live a godly life. Non-Christians often look at Christians as hypocritical because we say one thing but do another. Show those close to you that you care, spend time with them, help meet their needs, and offer to listen when they have problems. You might not be able to answer all their questions, but they can't deny the reality of what Christ has done in your life. If you find this is hard to do, perhaps God is speaking to you about your own need to "walk more closely with Him every day." Another important part of sharing your faith is to pray for those you interact with. If you can't think of anyone who isn't a Christian, pray for God to place someone in your life who needs him.

Also make a habit of reading the Bible, praying, and going to church. These things shouldn't be done for attention or for the sake of doing them, but to help you "grow in your own faith." Being passionate about Christ will help others see that there's something different about you, and they will want to know what it is. You can also reflect Christ through kind words, patience, a gentle temperament, choosing to love even difficult people, carefully monitoring what you watch or listen to, and treating others with respect.

There is a specific time when you first realized your need of a Savior. Then when you heard that there was one, you rejoiced, repented of wrongdoings, and believed. It could be a memorable day or simply a certain expanse of time in your life. Think back. When was it for you?

Were you addicted to drugs or alcohol and found a Savior who helped you to break free? Were you severely depressed and found a Savior who gave you hope to continue onward? Did you get in trouble with the law and then realize just how much you had messed your life up? Did you miss out on some seemingly wonderful opportunity but then realized that things would work out okay anyway because there is a God that loved you?

At some point, you realized that life wasn't working out so well when you were running it on your own and you needed help. People can usually run their lives okay when things are going well, but when the inevitable problems happen, we need help to see another perspective.

Your testimony may have been extreme and radical, or it might have been a calm profession of true belief. Both testimonies depict God's love and mercy because all (both loud and quiet sinners) have sinned and fallen short of the glory of God.

Another reason to share my testimony is because God tells me to. 1 Peter 3:15–16 reads,

> But in your hearts revere Christ as Lord. Always be prepared to give an answer to every-

> one who asks you to give the reason for the hope that you have. But do this with gentleness and respect, keeping a clear conscience, so that those who speak maliciously against your good behavior in Christ may be ashamed of their slander.

This verse reminds me to worship Christ as Lord of my life, and if someone asks about my hope as a believer, always be ready to explain it in a gentle and respectful way.

A testimony is a story and we all love stories. We go to the movies, we watch television, and we read books to hear about great stories. Stories can give us experiences to emulate. They can show us people to relate to and root for. They also give us the opportunity to see from another person's point of view.

We long to see superheroes saving people. We enjoy seeing two people find each other and fall in love. We watch people go to other countries and have different experiences. We even find it interesting to see someone's adventures in space or on another planet. Yes, stories help us see beyond our own little world.

In speaking about what God has done in my life, I am also remembering all of God's goodness. When I recount what he has done in the past, it gives me even more faith and courage for present living.

When the Israelites remembered all that God had done in the past when he brought them out of Egypt, they had courage to continue onward into the promised land. When Jesus's disciples thought back on all he had taught them, they were able to spread Jesus's Way to more and more people. Remembering their life before Jesus and comparing it to their lives after knowing Jesus spurred them on.

The more we're honest about mistakes we've made in the past, the more other people can relate to us. There's a natural tendency to want to look as perfect as possible on the outside, so we hold past mistakes deep within us. Hiding things is a lie that keeps people at arm's length. Sharing brings them closer into intimate and real conversations.

Testimonies from Colleagues

Greg,

> First, thank you for allowing God to use you for sending out the daily bread for so long. I love that you are dedicated, and it's super encouraging every week. I'm encouraged to look into doing something similar.

*****

Hello all,

A fellow employee's mom is undergoing blood work and test to see if her leukemia (CCL) has returned. Sadly, her doctors suspect it has, but will not be able to confirm until her bone marrow biopsy results come back. She came to me this afternoon asking the Daily Bread family to pray for her mom. I know Jesus is a healer and deliverer, and her mom will be just fine.

*****

Greg,

Thanks for the prayers of the Daily Bread family. I want to let you know Brad is back at work, after falling out a few days ago. It did not look good at the time he was rushed to the hospital. All praises to Jesus, the doctors found out it was a combination of meds the doctors put him on after a back procedure a few days ago. Thank you for praying for him.

*****

Hi Greg,

I have a prayer request that I feel the need to broadcast. My family and I have some very close friends that need some prayers. Their kids are like my kids and the reverse. Just after Christmas, the husband decided he was no longer in love with his wife and decided to move out. Obviously this was devastating to his wife and four kids, ages eight to eighteen and had a profound negative impact on all of them. The wife is saved and is a devoted Christian and has been doing all she can to trust Jesus and per her future and that of her kids, in his hands, knowing Jesus will not leave her at a time like this. She has found great comfort in her job as an elementary school teacher, but unfortunately she was told the other day that her contract for next year will not be renewed. She's in an even deeper state of depression and trying to hold onto God's unchanging hand. Thanks for the Daily Bread family's prayers, asking for God to lead and guide the whole family on the path he wants for their lives.

*****

Hi Greg,

I have a prayer request. As you may know, my mom Debbie has been battling a fight with cancer. Through lots of prayer, she has been healing! God is so good! She is finally out of the hospital for a week and a half. I got a chance to see her this weekend, and she is getting around pretty well with her walker. This is significant improvement since the last time I saw her, and she was just taking her first steps after being completely bedridden for a month and in the hospital for a long two months with various complications. It is a true testimony of prayer that she is even with us today! On Monday, 2/20/19, she will be going for her PET scan. I'm asking for the prayers of the Daily Bread family, knowing we will see yet another miracle in her healing and her scans come back clean and cancer free!

*****

Greg,

I would like to share the following: our life transformation may not be as quick or drastic. Still, as people notice how Christ's love is changing us over time, we'll have opportunities to tell others what Christ has done for us. I wonder how old I'll be when people notice that Christ has changed me. I tell others all the time what Christ has done for me, but my personality never has quite afforded me the opportunity for others to notice that I'm a Christian without putting it out there in front of them. I know through the prayers of others, God is not finished with me. Glory to his name!

*****

"I pray that you [will] grasp how wide and long and high and deep is the love of Christ" (Ephesians 3:17–18).

Yes! This also rings true for the PET scans I endured throughout my chemo and will have repeatedly going forward. I had such an intense fear gripping me as the bed initially moved into the machine, and then I was able to let that fear go and had the weirdest sense of calm take over throughout the remaining sixteen minutes I was in the machine each time. Amazing things happen when you let go and let God. Another great message today, Greg.

*****

"All the days ordained for me were written in your book before one of them came to be" (Psalms 139:16).

This one resonated with me today. Thank you! I've been trying not to dwell on why I had a cancer diagnosis this year, but more or so think on why I was given a second chance and what I'm meant to do with it. Great message today.

*****

"What has happened to me has actually served to advance the gospel (Philippians 1:12)"

A friend named Roberto is going to have LASIK surgery, asking for prayers that all goes well, knowing God is in control of all things. I have a friend Maritza who has cancer and is not doing well. She needs prayer to see if she is a candidate for a clinical trial, and it is her last hope. I put her in God's hands, for he alone can heal like no other.

*****

To all the Daily Bread family,

"Immediately Jesus reached out his hand and caught him" (Matthew 14:31).

This was meant for me today, knowing I'm in safe hands all day and night.

*****

"May the God of hope fill you with all joy and peace as you trust in him" (Romans 15:13).

Thank you, Greg, for always sending out the Daily Bread! I ask for a prayer request. I can't go into details, but the Lord knows exactly what it is. I ask for calmness, favor, and composure for this situation that I'm about to face today. I believe in the power of prayer, knowing that God is

> the author and finisher of my life, and I already have other real close friends praying on my behalf. You are the first person I asked, and the Lord knows why he has set this day, maybe for such a time as this. God bless you! Esther.

I give God all the praise and glory for the few testimonies shared in this book. Your story can be a key to unlock someone else's prison. God uses people as his hands and feet.

The more I tell my story of my initial meeting with Christ, the more I keep that first love feeling alive. Revelations tells me that it's possible for me to do good work, have patient endurance, not tolerate evil, and even suffer for my faith in Christ and yet still be missing something if I've lost my first love. The love of Christ should be my motive for doing good works and pressing on in the faith. Speaking often about my salvation experience keeps that first love feeling alive. I remember when I first really loved God and why.

As God teaches me more and more, I will gain other testimonies besides my initial salvation one. As I apply God's Truth to my life, I will have many more testimonies about him—testimonies that God's way really is the Way.

God is working within me every day and slowly changing me to be more like him in the fruit of the

Spirit—love, joy, peace, patience, kindness, goodness, faithfulness, gentleness, and self-control. My full testimony doesn't end until I exit this earthly life. So I desire to share it all, every single way that I see God active in my life.

The Apostle Paul reiterates this in Philippians 1:12 when he says that he wants you to know that everything that has happened to him has helped him to spread the good news.

CHAPTER 5

Receiving Our Daily Bread (God's Word)

It is an amazing thing that God reveals himself to us by speaking.

Before we identify God's Word with a leather-bound Bible, first consider the concept of God speaking. He communicates himself—he reveals and expresses himself to humanity, not simply in a proposition, but in a person. That's why Jesus is called *the Word*. "In the beginning was the Word and the Word was with God and the Word was toward God, he was in the beginning with God." Jesus is the full embodiment of God's Word. When God has something to say—something to reveal, something to communicate to humanity—he reveals it in the God-man, Jesus. He is the climactic expression of God's Word, the Word *incarnate*.

But there's also the Word spoken. This is the way that Word is used most in the New Testament. Again and again, we find out that the Word (or the message of the gospel) is what has come to people and been embraced for salvation. People have heard and believed this message about Jesus. So it's not just this personal Jesus about whom we can make up our own message about. There's a very particular message—a particular work and message—that goes with this person, Jesus. They're bound up together. So the gospel word is essential to what God is communicating to humanity and expressing about himself.

Finally, there's the word written. This is the word in scripture, the Bible. How do we access the Word incarnate and the word spoken? We do so through the word written. That's what God has given us this side of heaven. He has given us his word written to access the true message of the gospel and to access Jesus himself as the full expression of God's Word.

God sometimes communicates with people on earth by speaking directly to them. These can be called instances of God's Word of personal address. Examples are found throughout scripture. At the very beginning of creation, God speaks to Adam, "And the Lord God commanded the man, saying, You may freely eat of every tree of the garden; but of the tree of the knowledge of good and evil you shall not eat, for, for in the day that you eat of it you shall die" (Genesis 2:16–17). After the sin of Adam and Eve, God stills comes and speaks directly and personally to them in the words of the curse (Genesis 3:16–19). Another prominent example of God's direct personal address to people on earth is found in the giving of the Ten Commandments, "And God spoke all these words, saying, I am the Lord your God, who brought you out of the land of Egypt, out of the house of bondage. You shall have no other gods before me" (Exodus 20:1–3).

But how do we take in God's Word? Let me give you three categories for how we receive his Word as we begin to develop various habits of grace. The *first* is reading the Word. We read the Word when we take it in real time. Whether someone else is reading it and we're hearing it, or whether we're reading it with our own eyes, taking it in at regular speed, that's reading the Word.

Second, studying is where we slow down, ask questions, try to put pieces together, and see what we're not getting when we're reading. If the Bible really is a book from God, it wouldn't make sense for us humans to understand every word of it the first time we heard it. For your whole life, there will be things that you don't understand in the Bible. So study is the way that we engage with it, the way we slow down and try to figure out answers to questions we have so we can better understand what we're reading.

Finally, the *third* category is meditation. Meditation is much underrated, it's often forgotten, and it's actually the way that the Bible talks most often about how we are supposed to receive God's Word. Reading gets it into our heads, study clarifies the meaning, but meditation is when we chew on what God has said, when we marvel at it, and when we apply it to our hearts. The highest point of hearing God's Word or taking in the Bible is meditation.

When it comes to reading and studying the Bible, we want to move toward the enjoyment of Jesus in the Word, toward marveling, toward being astounded by him.

Another way to put it this—reading is like watching a movie in real time. Study is like slowing it down, going into slo-mo, watching where the computer-generated graphics are, where the person is coming in and out of the frame. It's about trying to slow it down and understand everything a bit better. Meditation is like a freeze-frame. At a great moment, you pause the movie and reflect on what's happened in the story. You reflect on that one moment and *appreciate* what's happening.

To put it yet another way—reading is like surveying a forest. Study is like finding a tree and chopping it up into logs. Meditation is like putting them on a fire, in a nice cozy cabin, and enjoying the warmth in the middle of a cold Minnesota winter.

What about application? I would say that the way you engage in application in Bible meditation is by applying it to your heart. Try to apply it to your heart every day. Don't circumvent the heart and go straight from the head in reading and studying to external actions. Go from taking in the Bible to applying it to your heart in meditation and then let the good deeds flow. God will change our external lives in his perfect timing as his Word is applied to our hearts in meditation.

As you seek to cultivate your own "habits of grace," I would encourage you to think outside the box when it comes to Bible intake. Receiving God's word—hearing his voice in the scriptures—isn't just sitting at a desk and reading a Bible (though it can be that), or sitting at a desk with a pen or pencil doing a study. It could also be hearing God's Word read aloud. It could be biblically faithful preaching. It could also be biblically faithful books, articles, or other types of media. And most important of all, it is doing what it takes to pause and ponder, to stop and chew, to seek to apply God's revealed truth to the your heart through meditation.

CHAPTER 6

It's All in the Bread (God's Word)

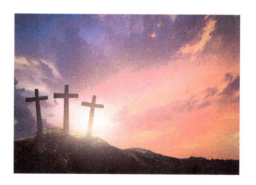

I realize as an adult, God's Word is active and alive in my life. I turn around to look for answers and questions not realizing it's all in God's Word.

The very heart of this Bible from Genesis to Revelation is the fact that Jesus Christ is God's Son. Take that by faith, that he was born of the Virgin

Mary and that he died on the cross for a special purpose. It wasn't just death because he was put to death by the Romans. You and I put him to death. I helped my sins. The Bible says that God took all of our sins and laid them on him. And it was my sins, your sins, the whole world, that nailed him to the cross. But in that cross, a great victory came. The Bible tells us that Jesus Christ triumphed over sin and death and the grave and hell and there is hope today—security, peace, and assurance—in coming to the cross.

But the first step that you must take is a childlike step. It's a simple step, so simple that many will rebel at it. It's so simple that you may reject it. In fact, the Bible says thousands of people stumble over it because it is so simple—because you see, the man with his PhD has to come like a little child exactly the same way. And that's hard for a businessman, socialite, union leader, showperson, or journalists to do. We don't like to humble ourselves and become small and just come with simple childlike faith. But when you do, your life is changed. Believe that and accept him by faith into your heart.

But you have to be willing to give up your sins. Repentance means that you acknowledge that you have sinned and that you are willing to turn from them, and if you are willing, you come by faith to Christ, and he will give you a new life. And it becomes God's life because the Bible says that God exists from eternity to eternity. Eternal life begins at the moment you receive Christ. It's a new dimension of living.

We have third dimension. We're talking about fourth dimension. But I tell you there's another dimension—it's the spiritual dimension that thousands in America have not tried. It's the dimension revealed in this Book (the bible), the dimension that Jesus Christ offers free to everyone who will trust him.

Many people read the Bible as if it were fundamentally about us, our improvement, our life, our victory, our faith, our holiness, our godliness. We treat it like a disconnected series of timeless principles that will give us our best life now if we simply apply them. We read it, in other words, as if it were a heaven-sent self-help manual, a divinely delivered to-do list. But by reading the Bible this way, we, like the two companions on the road to Emmaus, totally miss the point. As Luke 24 shows, it's possible to read the Bible, study the Bible—even memorize large portions of the Bible—and miss the main point of the Bible. In fact, unless we go to the Bible to see Jesus and his work for us, even devout Bible reading can become fuel for our own self-improvement plans, a source for the help we need to conquer today's challenges and take control of our lives.

God's goal in speaking to us in the Bible is profound, but not complicated. In fact, we can say that all of God's Word comes to us in two words. And if we are going to understand the Bible rightly, we have to be able to distinguish properly between these two words.

The Bible, which is the Word of God, provides the basis for all our teaching and living, so it is very important and relevant in today's world to us.

We know many people who believe that everything in life is relative, that it is just all a matter of opinion. For Lutherans, however, the most important "opinion" is God's—he is the only absolute, and everything is relative to him. We look to the Bible to give us something solid that we can point to as a standard outside our own sinful thinking.

There are some people who will not understand this. There are those who think that the Bible is just a book of stories. As a Lutheran, we need to believe it is much, much more.

The Bible is a collection of sixty-six books written by many different people over thousands of years in Hebrew, Aramaic, and Greek. The type of literature varies, history, prophecy, poetry, speeches, and letters. The Bible is considered a masterpiece of literature.

The remarkable thing about the Bible is that it was written not only by humans but also by God. So God is the Author behind the authors. For the Bible is God's Word, then God would have to be the real Author, the Authority behind it. This is what is meant when Christians say the Bible is "inspired by God." The Holy Spirit inspired, "breathed-in," or carried along these various writers as they wrote so that they produced more than just human writings or stories. In fact, these writers conveyed the very Word of God.

When we Christians say the three main slogans of our belief, "scripture alone," "grace alone," and "faith alone," we are saying, for the "scripture alone" slogan, that the Bible is the final determining factor in what we believe and teach in the church. Scripture is not joined with church tradition, human reason or experience, or anything else. "Scripture alone!"

We see the Bible as part of the third commandment. Martin Luther says in the third commandment, "We should fear and love God so that we do not despise preaching and His Word, but hold it sacred and gladly hear and learn it." To "hold it sacred" means to see the Bible as holy. Because it is associated with God, and God is holy, we therefore call the Bible the "Holy Bible."

So why is the Word of God important? Because it is "God inspired, God breathed, Sacred and Holy." And why is that so special for all Christians to believe? It is all true and that "God's Word endures forever!" Amen.

A PRAYER OF SALVATION

Lord Jesus, I pray, for whoever reads this book and do not know you for the pardoning of their sins, that they will accept you as Lord and Savior today.

The Bible, all sixty-six books, reveals a common thread—redemption through the shed blood of Jesus Christ. By faith in Christ alone, today you can receive him as your Lord and Savior, turning from your sins in order to pursue his will.

You can do this right now. You can have abundant and eternal life if you will surrender to Christ.

REFERENCES

Billy Graham
Chaplain Barry C. Black
Christianity Today
Grudem, Wayne. *Systematic Theology.*
Crossway.org

ABOUT THE AUTHOR

Gregory J. Holt was born on November 23, 1962, in Metropolitan Hospital in New York City. He was raised in foster care, not knowing any of his parents. Being a child of the State of New York, he and his brother always packed their bags and moved on to the next family. It seems the author never had a stable upbringing as a child; some families were abusive, while some were loving. He thanks God for having his hands on him as a child.

The author graduated high school in Queens and went to New York Tech College in Brooklyn. Then he attended Delhi University in upstate New York. He met his wife in New York, and they were married on April 10, 1987. They decided to leave New York City and move to Baltimore, Maryland, where they lived for twenty years.

In 2006, they decided to move to Phoenix, Arizona, where the author was baptized and was ordained to be a deacon and was called to the ministry to preach his Word.

The author's department that he worked in was relocated to El Paso, Texas. Then he was given the opportunity to transfer to their Orlando, Florida, location. In 2015, he and his wife moved to Florida, where they found an awesome church and where God is using them mightily for his service.

"For I know the plans I have for you, declares the Lord, plans to prosper you and not to harm you, plans to give you hope and a future" (Jeremiah 29:11).